Life Is Not Good
Ethical Antinatalism in Haiku

Dan Dana

Five Palms Press
Sarasota, Florida, USA
dandana.us/fivepalms

Cover photo: The author in his father's arms, November 1945

Contents

Preface

Antinatalism

we seldom ask why
life's bowl of tasty cherries
enjoyed by so few?

pain trumps pleasure on
world's unbalanced balance sheet,
ask evil's victims

animal cousins
suffer death by predator,
or meat factory

evolution's tool:
pain serves genome's goal, not ours,
in life's lethal game

ethicists debate,
consensus does not mean truth,
paradigms can shift

Image: Antinatalism International

Introduction

Is your life good?

Then you are among the lucky few sentient creatures (humans are just *one* species that feels pain) happily living a life of abundant pleasure. Count your blessings. Thank your lucky stars. Please don't forget the others.

Every act that prevents a human birth, particularly an unchosen one, may save innumerable future lives from anguish and death throughout the remaining four billion years that sentient life will inhabit this planet. We tend to reproduce.

We can never know who those nulled beings might have been, but their lives would have been as real to them as yours and mine are to us today—and likely far less fortunate. They will never exist, so cannot thank us for sparing them a life of woe. Preventing a life of misery is the most generous anonymous gift we can give.

This is ethical antinatalism.

Read on. But be forewarned: Your bedrock assumptions may be shaken. Prepare to face the ethical dilemma we find ourselves in simply by being alive in an unjust world. As humans, we uniquely possess the power of moral choice, and its attendant responsibilities. What to do with that power?

5

I. Two Words to Know

#1: <u>Antinatalism</u> is a compassionate humanistic philosophy that values prevention of human and non-human suffering above the purported inherent goodness of life. Many readers may initially recoil in moral revulsion from the titular premise of this book: *Life Is Not Good.* Let me explain.

For centuries, religious doctrines have infused their adherents' popular cultures with the alternative belief: Life is inherently *good*—hence our fervent efforts to save lives, our joy upon hearing that a new baby has arrived, and our compelling impulse to avoid or delay one's own death. Indeed, religions generally view life as innately sacred, a gift from God, without regard for the hedonic quality of that life. We naively assume that the new life's joys and pleasures will beat the odds by outweighing its suffering and pain. Further, we seldom think about the quality of *future* lives (each of which will end in certain death) that may descend from this celebrated newborn for thousands or millions of years.

Sadly, life's lottery is stacked against such wishes.

Antinatalism, a logical extension of secular humanism, holds that if the latter (pain) exceeds the former (pleasure) across the entire present and future population of sentient creatures on Earth, then life is, by definition, *not* good. If that imbalance is extreme, one may reasonably question whether "more time on the cross" (to apply a Christian meme) is desirable, individually or population-wide. This question is especially intimate in the case of terminally ill persons who are suffering unrelievable pain with no hope of recovery.

We mercifully "put down" beloved pets, race horses, and other non-human sentient beings to spare them further suffering. Humans, believed by the religious to possess an immaterial "soul," are generally barred, in most jurisdictions, from lawfully choosing that merciful course for themselves.

To pose the question globally, is life on Earth a good thing or a bad thing? Life's earliest form arose some 3.5 billion years ago. It is certain to end some five billion years hence as the sun's fusion reactor exhausts its supply of hydrogen fuel and expands to our planet's orbit, vaporizing this watery orb, even its rocky core. Our violent end may be met even earlier by some other cataclysmic astronomical event—many such hazards lurk Earth's fragile place in space.

Meanwhile, are we a *lucky* planet, comfortably situated at a goldilocks distance from our star where surface liquid water makes sentient life, as we know it, possible? Or, are the lifeless planets in our solar system the lucky ones? I will poetically explore this question in "Say It in Haiku" below.

Galactically and beyond, where astrobiologists estimate that sentient life exists on countless millions of host planets and moons, should we wish upon their hapless denizens the fate that has befallen our blue marble? Any life forms found elsewhere may be unrecognizably different from those that populate our planet, but evolution by natural selection is surely the mechanism by which ecological adaptation and speciation occur wherever life may emerge from abiological matter.

Sentience would presumably follow in due time—in Earth's history, over one billion years transpired from the initial emergence of single-cell life until multi-cellular organisms appeared. Sentient mammals evolved from Triassic reptiles after another two billion years. Humans have been present for 0.000001% of the span of life's existence on Earth. A wide lens reveals that the question is immensely broader than whether you and I are enjoying this sunny day and this privileged lifetime.

In these pages, I invite readers to re-think the common assumption that life is inherently good. Let us consider the sum and balance of its hedonic components: pleasure and pain, loosely defined. In the final section, I list some actionable steps that empathetic individuals may take to put this humanistic worldview into practice.

#2: <u>**Haiku**</u> is an ancient form of Japanese poetry consisting of three unrhymed lines, each having five, seven, and five syllables respectively. The bulk of this book is written in the adapted form "haiku quintets"—five stanzas of haiku having a common topical theme. A photo or image illustrates and completes the finished piece.

I devised this novel poetic structure as my preferred tool for conveying a compact understanding of a particular concept or sentiment, here related to antinatalism. Further examples of its use may be found in my previous books of haiku quintets listed at the end of this volume.

II. My Path to Antinatalism

I grew up on a farm in the American Midwest. Each spring we scoured our pastures and brushy woodland on horseback, rounding up the cows and calves. Once all the cattle were corralled, the calves born since last year's round-up were separated from their mothers. We would then "work" the yearlings.

This involved several excruciatingly painful steps. They were branded as property of our family farm. My job, as the youngest "man" (actually adolescent boy and early teen) on the team, was to keep the open woodfire stoked and the branding iron red-hot. The smell of burned hair and flesh remains seared in my memory, along with the guttural sounds uttered by the calves as the sizzling branding iron pressed against their hindquarters.

The bull calves were castrated, their testicles tossed aside on the ground. I gathered them into a bucket. Next morning, my mom sliced and fried these "Rocky Mountain oysters" in butter for breakfast with eggs and toast. I admit, they were tasty.

Vaccines were injected with an 18-gauge needle. Large pills to prevent common bovine diseases were inserted with a bolus gun into their throats. These were the least painful steps in the process, judging from the calves' reactions.

Dehorning was the worst. The calves bellowed (screamed) in agony as chunks of skull were cut out around their budding horns with a cup dehorner, without anesthetic. Their eyes widened and bulged in shock and pain. I was sickened as these innocent, helpless, gentle creatures were tortured as I watched. I was complicit.

At the time, I understood this treatment was necessary to prepare the animal as a source of meat. My family sold them to feedlot operators for fattening before slaughter. We kept one calf to butcher for our own table. The selected animal was taken by pick-up truck to a local butchery for processing. I witnessed the calf being shot between the eyes with a rifle, causing it to slump to the ground. Its carcass was promptly skinned and carved into steaks and other cuts of meat neatly wrapped and frozen in packages for our dinner table over coming months.

On one particular occasion, I hand-fed a Hereford bobby (orphaned) calf in a barn adjacent to our house. This twice-daily visit produced an affectionate familiarity resembling friendship with the calf, whom I had named "Shortstuff." I routinely spoke to him during his feedings. He trusted me and enjoyed having his ears, face, and back rubbed. I hugged his warm neck, nuzzling his redolent fur. I loved him. I sobbed as Shortstuff was loaded into the truck bound for slaughter. On that day, I could not bear to go along to witness his murder.

Throughout the process, from rounding up the young cattle to carving them into edible pieces, the men who performed these tasks seemed unbothered by the pain they inflicted. It seemed their work was as impersonal as growing crops of insensate grain. (To be fair, my older brother recently admitted to feeling squeamish about the hurt we inflicted, but accepted the necessity of it—he remains a farmer today.) Nazi guards at death camps may have regarded their "work" as equally impersonal. As a young boy of delicate sensibilities, I could not refrain from vividly imagining our animals' pain.

Although there were other aspects of farm labor that I did not enjoy, working the cattle was perhaps the part that decisively compelled me to seek another career. As the youngest member of my family, I had simply assumed that I would grow up, marry, have children, and continue the generational cycle. But I became increasingly worried that I was not emotionally capable of doing what would be required of me.

In the summer of 1962, on the precipice of adulthood, I reached an inflection point:

Mowing Alfalfa

that pivotal day
summer before senior year
"to farm" was my plan

mowing alfalfa
was my chore, and my future
by noon, life transformed

lightning struck that day
a jolt of empowerment:
"I can change the plan!"

dropping FFA
enrolling at Ole Mizzou
my new field was math

fickle plans took me
through six rewarding decades
to greener pastures

Photo credit: youtube (similar tractor and mower)

As my education and career in my chosen "helping profession" (eventually, mediation) progressed, my worldview expanded to new horizons. I learned of historical and present-day events of indescribable human suffering. Images of the Nazi holocaust, torturous executions, battlefield carnage, slavery, and mass starvation of children tore at my conscience. Myriad more examples of human cruelty could be listed here—indeed, too many to bear. How could such brutality happen in the same world as mine, even at this very moment as I write these words?

A visit to a Nazi extermination camp in 2022 made this reality searingly vivid:

Struthof

soaring overhead,
white dove's feathered innocence
at a safe remove

watching "pieces" crawl
up icy steps for roll call,
then falter and die

smelling stench of death,
of their shit, of rotting flesh,
of chimney's vile fumes

shaming my own kind,
"Honor and Homeland" calls us
to fight obscene wars

no dove's innocence—
nationalism is poison,
humanity's curse

Photo 22 September 2022: Shadow selfie between double barbed wire fence surrounding prison where 22,000 victims of nationalism died 1941-1944, Natzwiller-Struthof, Nazi-occupied France

In college I learned that Homo sapiens is just another species of mammal, sharing much DNA and many biological characteristics with our mammal cousins, as well as with contemporary non-mammalian species with whom we share ancestry. Among those characteristics is the capacity to experience pain and the fear of pain.

A key difference between those species and our own is that so-called "lower" animals cannot tell us that it hurts in *our* language. We do not—or choose to not—understand *their* language. We treat them as inanimate objects, not as fellow sentient creatures who experience pleasure and pain as we do—a tragic failure of empathy.

Evolution by natural selection, the central tool of biology, developed and employs the sensation of pain to incentivize individuals to avoid predators and other risks to survival as a reproducing member of our species. Evolution's concern is not for our personal health and happiness; rather, its natural intelligence "cares" only about the survival and success of our genome in the fiercely competitive "dog eat dog" business of life on Earth.

We are omnivorous creatures, historically feeding on the flesh of our fellow sentient beings. Our "selfish genes," as biologist Richard Dawkins explains, drive procreative and social behavior. Our smug notions of autonomy and self-determination are largely illusory—the "self-made man" is a myth. Our genes sit in the driver's seat, taking us for a ride, indifferent to the hedonic quality of our lives.

In sociobiological terms, our utility to humankind is solely to ensure survival of our species—our suffering as individuals is of no concern in this merciless biosphere. We exist as instruments of our genome. We turn to our friends and our gods for solace, deflecting attention from our existential insignificance in the infinity of time and space. Meanwhile, we enjoy the one life we are allotted to the best of our ability, and as good fortune allows.

Personally, I find my accidental existence a source of awe, meaning, and pleasure. I'm among the lucky ones who have not suffered the horrors mentioned above. By pure happenstance, my life is good.

Nature's Killing Machine

being begets pain,
our planet hosts misery,
birth damns us to life

food animals live
lives of torture and torment,
endless holocaust

human hierarchies
bring wars, tyrants, hunger, death,
wielding leaders' club

I'm a tiny cog
in nature's killing machine,
evolution's craft

does joie de vivre
outweigh constant suffering
on life's balance scale?

Photo: NASA. All sentient creatures, their suffering, and their remorseless exploitation, occur on the thin veneer of our planet, a global killing field.

Along the way, I discarded the supernaturalism of my childhood religion, a conceit that life is something special, more than a particular composition of matter. I learned that we living things are a biological phenomenon evolving from organic components by natural selection—nature's genius did not require supernatural intervention to create us. Memes taught in Sunday school, such as "God is good," "life is sacred," and "heaven awaits the faithful," did not hold up to even rudimentary scientific scrutiny.

I Tried

I read the bible,
I listened to Pastor Bob,
I pushed down my doubts

each Sunday morning
I sat still, as expected,
waiting for the light

Jews are confident,
Catholics are sure they're right,
Muslims too, I'm told

Mom said to trust God
I feared the torture of Hell
"could I deserve that?"

my young faith faltered,
I tried to make sense of it
in the end, I failed

Photo: The abandoned church of my childhood, Knoxville, Missouri, March 15, 2022

Bertrand Russell

your words set me free
scales fell from wondering eyes
young life's course re-set

superstitions foiled
country church's hold released
dogma's chains broken

freethought flowed freely
in secular humanism's
sensible worldview

these sixty years past
I ponder the Universe
in your wise shadow

your book made me me
enriched life beyond measure
thank you, Lord Russell

Photo: Original copy of the book that changed my life in 1961

Christian Cosmologists

that most odd creature,
the "Christian Cosmologist,"
should now be extinct

but specimens live,
defying laws of physics,
though sightings are rare

perhaps they possess
supernatural power
over reason's rules?

I'm a stern skeptic
of my own cozy beliefs,
self-deception's tricks

as a scientist*
I ask, where's the evidence?
show me it's not myth

* I'm a curious hobbyist, not a practicing researcher.

My 2014 e-book asks professional clergy, of any doctrine, to explain how their particular faith reconciles settled (i.e., noncontroversial) science with the basic tenets of their religion (i.e., supernatural deities and afterlife). So far, none have adequately responded. I tentatively conclude that one can either hold religious faith or accept the confirmed findings of science, but not both.

Secular Humanists

we care for people
in their natural lifetimes
we're good without gods

blind faith cannot see
ancient myths cloud our vision
of plain facts of life

inconvenient truth:
gods' will and heaven's gate are
pre-science fake news

we're born, then we die
savor this one awesome trip
smell sweet roses' scent

en route, please be kind
love our fellow passengers
aboard this frail boat

Photo: loupiote

If you have an appetite for further debunking of religion, see my books *Science and Secularism* and *The Reason Revolution: Atheism, Secular Humanism, and the Collapse of Religion*. In them, I argue for separation of church and state, and quixotically aspire to the eventual collapse of religion under the weight of its own illogic—a kinder, gentler humanity would surely result. Science is progressively supplanting the occult as we seek to understand the universe we live in. Long live science education!

Admittedly, full understanding of the biology of consciousness has yet to be achieved. Serious scholars may disagree, but few dispute that awareness is a *natural* phenomenon, not a *super*natural one, and is therefore subject to investigation and discovery by science.

Mysteries are regularly solved by empirical inquiry. The gods of the ancients, with their quaint creation myths and fervent hope for death-defying afterlife, have been abandoned to history books. Contemporary religions will surely join them in due time.

But I digress. Returning to our subject, I regard a secular humanist worldview as foundational to fully recognizing the ethical virtue of antinatalism. Religionists, who imagine supernatural features of existence such as metaphysical deities and conscious afterlife, will surely dismiss it as an unholy theory that is inconsistent with their traditional divinely inspired dogma.

Set aside your childhood's faith for a few pages. Consider this bold perspective—for the betterment of life on earth.

During my college years, distress about being part of a world where horrific and unstoppable misery is on-going and ever-present played a role in my youthful existential crisis.

A Decision Deferred

failing socially
failing academically
failing with women

my future seemed bleak
happiness felt beyond reach
I despaired of hope

a flash of insight
one day brightened my dark sky
—I could end my life!

I'd found a way out
of my doom's dreary prison
I was free to choose!

so ... do it today?
there's no rush, I decided
—and there still isn't

Setting: Freshman year at University of Missouri, 1963-64
Photo: On a return visit to campus with wife Susan, 2019

Consider these grim snippets selected from my memoir, *A Life Mostly Lived:*

Our Phylum's Caste System

Earth's vast common ground
shared with lower caste cousins,
our mammal kinfolk

all eat, drink, scratch, play,
carnal needs frustrate, delight,
all pee, poop, nest, sleep

our tribe hides in clothes,
boasting pompous pretentions
of upper caste rank

all feel pain, fear, love
their emotions mirror ours,
yet we torture them

may kindness bridge caste,
phylum's godless humanists
live the Golden Rule

Given that natural selection is an immutable feature of speciation, carnivores must be granted a waiver from the Golden Rule. Human omnivores, uniquely, have a moral choice. Many non-vegans, such as the author, lamely lament the tortuous treatment of our food animals. Photo: A mother loving her newborns, Connecticut, 27 April 2023

As We're Told

he dropped fiery death
on Japan's powerless pawns,
as Truman ordered

he showered vile gas
on trainloads of marked scapegoats,
as the Fuhrer wished

he launched cruise missiles
striking hospitals and schools,
as Putin desired

Members cast floor votes
to rescind democracy,
as Trump demanded

whether we believe
our duties serve greater good,
we do as we're told

Photo: 29 September 2022, Smithsonian Museum, Chantilly, Virginia.
The Enola Gay delivered "Little Boy" to Hiroshima 6 August 1945.

Paul

his tears spoke volumes
over goulash and salad
we listened, entranced

tender child of eight
survived Budapest ghetto's
merciless Nazis

ninety starving Jews
stuffed in freezing two-room flat
slept while standing up

winter without shoes,
people robbed of their clothing
on the streets at night

lions kill to eat,
but wild beasts are not cruel
—that's a human thing

Photo: Paul at our dinner table 10 December 2022

Afghan Girl

school was your way out
what horrid fate awaits you?
Taliban returns

hope fades from your dreams
your burqa hides your anguish
your unborn goals snuffed

girls' lives don't matter
misogyny rules your land
gender apartheid

mosque-state flogs reason
theocrats dictate your rights
Allah's enforcers

Levant's ancient myths
God's most cruel cult prevailed
girls' epic bad luck

At the time of this writing (15 July 2021), the Taliban was aggressively reestablishing control in Afghanistan following withdrawal of American forces. Photo: CNN

Watching War Begin

we stand on the bank
of Ukraine's river of blood
awaiting Putin

his fragile ego
breeds deranged lust to rebuild
Soviet glory

at what human cost?
horrific suffering pays
toxic hubris' toll

did the sweet scent of
the Orange Revolution
merely pause this stench?

shall evil prevail?
today we see fate's answer,
watching war begin

Screenshot 23 February 2022, minutes after Russia launched attack

I'll not belabor the point further. On the whole, the world is a nasty place for the vast majority of sentient creatures, human and non-human, a condition succinctly captured by the glib phrase "life sucks and then you die." Indeed, you and I, dear reader, are among the lucky few creatures on this planet who might legitimately claim that "life is good." We seldom reflect upon the perpetual worldwide holocaust going on around us, much of it at our own economic behest. In any case, there seems little that we, as mere cogs in the global wheel, can do about it.

By my eighth decade of life, I arrived at a philosophical position originating in ancient Greece and India termed "antinatalism"— the idea that the amount of pain and suffering experienced by sentient creatures *as a whole* dwarfs the amount of joy and pleasure found in being alive, sentient, and sensate. See reading references at the end of this volume to broaden this view.

This ethically unjustifiable imbalance leads to the inescapable yet controversial conclusion that procreation is morally wrong in the long view. Birthing new sentient beings dooms those offspring, and the millions of generations who may follow them, to lives they did not choose to live. By creating them, we have unwittingly made that choice for them. They will die, indirectly, by our hand. They, and the hordes of their descendants over the remaining few billion years of our planet's habitable existence before being vaporized by our enlarging sun, will suffer the consequences.

Still, paradoxically, I love and cherish my grandchildren. My own baby picture garnishes the cover of this book. I celebrate my life of good fortune, yet can question whether my non-existence might have been better—if not for myself, then for my descendancy. I am both a product of my culture, and a sober critic of it.

Such is the irony of ethical antinatalism.

My Relief Generation

nearing the hand-off
of my lap with the baton
your turn has begun

our story's passed on
distant past to far future
one life at a time

shrouded in folklore
memory's fleeting half-life
decays to nothing

save this slim box of
Papi's memory snippets
for your relievers

as future unfurls
preserve your lap's key moments
—the relay goes on

From my memoir *A Life Mostly Lived*. Photo: 2006

III. Say It in Haiku

The following haiku quintets pose issues that high-empathy readers may wish to consider before impulsively rejecting this book's provocative thesis that, at macro scale across space and time, sentient life is not good.

The references listed on a later page offer armchair ethicists other resources to corroborate the antinatalist worldview.

If you accept its veracity but feel impotent to make a meaningful difference on the daunting expanse of our planetary killing field, see "What Can I Do?" below. Nulled descendants in the averted future would thank you if they could.

The Most Moral Choice

most living things die
by being eaten alive
by a predator

"selfish genes" don't care
about our petty comforts,
only our species

pain evolved to serve
the survival of our breed
at each one's expense

what is life's virtue
if its price is suffering
of sentient creatures?

our most moral choice:
bring no new life to the world,
break trauma's cycle

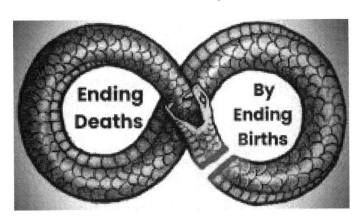

Image: Tamil Antinatalism

Descendancy

I fathered one child,
she has birthed two more new lives,
when will my line end?

if my clan extends,
descendants may witness our
planet's final days

my heirs will suffer
Earth's certain calamities
through millennia

untold extinctions
will spawn subspecies of us
—life will find a way

countless known unknowns
await the hapless creatures
I caused to exist

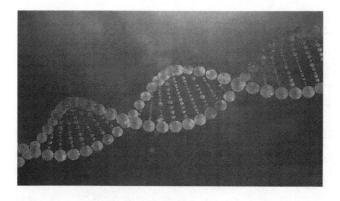

Image: Science Magazine

A Nulled Child Speaks

I was contraceived,
spared a life of misery,
I'll not beget more

poor Yoruba mom
forced by culture to give birth,
denied her due choice

she dreamed of freedom,
schooling, opportunity,
her stolen birthrights

but choice was restored,
countless unchosen lives were
averted today

a condom secured
the end of endless cycles
of faultless victims

Photo: Africa on-line

Poor Man's Philanthropy

man of modest means,
yet born of fate's lucky breaks,
seeks most bang for bucks

how to donate well,
do most good for my pittance?
—women control birth!

serves mom <u>and</u> nulled child,
no birth means no suffering,
generations hence

my small donation
yields compounding interest
for millennia

by preventing births
I can do philanthropy
like Rockefeller

Image: sopurple

Pathfinder International (pathfinder.org) allows targeted donation
for contraception and family planning.

Chicxulub Asteroid Impact

big day for Earth-life
sixty-six million years past,
brought mass extinction

mountain-size* space rock
thirty times a bullet's speed*
smashed Yucatan's shore

global firestorms raged,
tough birds, wee mammals eked out,
evolution worked

big dinos perished,
pre-chicken raptors survived,
and our parent shrews

lucky us, or not?
antinatalists wonder
when's the next big day?

* Six miles wide, 40,000 miles per hour

Image: New Scientist

Lucky Planet Mars

if all Earth's sentience
in one merciful instant
blinked out, no warning—

no more hunger, pain
no war, torture, mother's grief
no child's helpless cries

no shooter's hate crimes
no victim's screams of terror
no predator's bites

what pleasures and joys
of life's lottery winners
should warrant such hell?

cancel life's blueprint?
antinatalists' wonder:
lucky planet Mars?

Photo: Enviably lifeless surface of Mars (NASA)

Thin Silver Lining

a child's death grieves us,
loved ones left to mourn its loss,
a good life cut short

thin silver lining:
no generations follow,
countless lives unlived

progeny spared risks:
wars, misery, torment, fear,
in longtermism's view

would smiles outshine tears?
antinatalists question,
better not to live?

we fortunate few
know but this cloudless moment
in the roiling storm

Amazon

left a mere trickle
from high Andes' glacial melt
some two years ago

fell twelve thousand feet,
flowed four thousand winding miles,
birthing life on Earth

countless new species,
our family of cousins
draw breath from your flood

if life be thought good,
you're a god of genesis,
if bad, devil's twin

will your handiwork
survive mankind's blind mayhem?
our children shall see

Photo: On the Amazon near Macapá, Brazil, January 15, 2023

Climate Crisis

what to do, Earth-mates?
sacrifice for those to come?
hoard for our own time?

postpone certain doom?
New York, Shanghai sink,
drowning as forecast

migrants seek high ground,
famine, war, disease, typhoons,
death on epic scale

can globe act in time?
achieve planet-wide teamwork?
history says no

suffer Mars' harsh fate?
antinatalist dreamworld:
stillborn Pluto's peace

Photo: Pluto (NASA)

Mack's Vision

my sage age-peer friend
worried five decades ago,
foresaw grim future:

war, poverty, strife,
environmental collapse,
failed democracy

no child should suffer,
generations yet unborn
opt out fatherhood?

but Mack's wife had dreams:
family hearth, happy home
mother's vision reigned

"selfish genes" won debate
fate's sealed, progeny's in store
—grandfather of four

Image: pngtree

No Whining on the Yacht

we privileged few
by race, place, parental genes,
accidents of birth

hordes on leaky boats
face fear, hunger, pain, scorn, hell,
unfair privation

think of world's oppressed,
think of Afghan refugees,
and those left behind

unthinkable grief,
beyond our playground's border
—what can just one do?

at least we can be
kind, generous, meek, grateful
—don't whine on the yacht

Photo: unsplash

Palimpsest

boats lie at anchor,
palm fronds sway in morning breeze
this present moment

seas will rise and fall,
the landscape I view today
is a palimpsest

asteroids will strike,
ice ages, cataclysms span
geologic time

Earth will vaporize
as swelling sun consumes us
five billion years hence

as species evolve,
today's far future will be
their present moment

Photo: an ordinary Sarasota morning, 29 April 2016

A Whimsy of Fate

as a kid, I thought
my life would last forever,
death hid behind Now

grown, in the abstract,
I understood I will die
—a distant specter

now nearing eighty,
as my life's been mostly lived,
death's shroud is slipping

my mom, at ninety,
murmured "It went by so fast!"
she died the next day

on cosmic scale, I
accept my existence as
a whimsy of fate

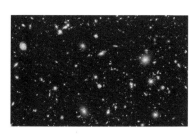

The observable Universe contains two trillion galaxies, each with millions of stars, each with its family of planets. Our eon began with the Big Bang 13.8 billion years ago. Per Physics Nobelist Roger Penrose, there may have been, and will be, an infinite number of eons. Life is an emergent natural phenomenon. We are not alone.

Photo: Ultra Deep Field by NASA's Webb Space Telescope. Most dots are galaxies, up to 13.2 billion lightyears away in space and time.

My Afterlife

my atoms will roam,
join other earth-bound life forms:
mouse, bird, fish, worm, weed

as dad, my genes will
walk, talk, think, feel, reproduce,
in my offspring's form

my molecules float
in air until Earth's end-time,
five billion years hence

sun's sons go nova
generations of star-stuff
I'm galaxy-wide

as teacher-writer,
some wise bits may last awhile
—perhaps this haiku?

Dan Dana

1945 September 23 – 20

Read my memoir
A Life Mostly Lived

IV. What Can I Do?

Are you still with me? This may have been a difficult trek for some readers through the saga of life's killing field to reach our journey's grim conclusion. I thank you for your emotional endurance and for your compassion for human and animal suffering.

More importantly, future generations may thank you if your conscience moves you to take any of these actions:

- Veganism/vegetarianism, or reduction in consumption of animal products
- Choosing to have no, or fewer, children
- Donating to charities that support women's contraceptive/ abortion choice
- Voting for political candidates who support abortion rights
- Activism for animal rights and against animal cruelty
- Neutering your pets.
- Activism to oppose religious promotion of large families
- Activism to repair the crumbling wall of separation between church and state
- Supporting science education and opposing faith-based schooling of children
- Voting for openly atheist political candidates, who will keep religion out of public policy
- Activism to normalize atheism in public discourse, reducing its pejorative connotation. If you're in the closet, come on out. The water's fine!

Author Bio

I am a retired mediator, psychologist, and educator living with wife Susan in Sarasota, Florida. Born in 1945 on a family farm in Missouri, I served, reluctantly, in the U.S. Army in Vietnam (non-combat) and Panama Canal Zone (1966-1968). Holding the PhD in psychology from University of Missouri (1977), I am the author of two books on mediation and one on secular humanism. Five Palms Press, named for my perch overlooking Sarasota Bay, was created to share my poetic handiwork in retirement. I am the father of one and grandfather of two.

Books by Dan Dana

The haiku quintet collection:

- *A Life Mostly Lived: True Stories in 85 Syllables*
- *Life Is Not Good: Antinatalism in Haiku*
- *Haiku Quintets*
- *Songs of the Pandemic*
- *Common Ground: Haiku, Mediation, and Police Reform*
- *Resisting Trumpism: Haiku Quintets*
- *Science and Secularism: Haiku Quintets and Other Musings*

Other works:

- *The Reason Revolution: Atheism, Secular Humanism, and the Collapse of Religion*
- *Conflict Resolution: Mediation Tools for Everyday Worklife*
- *Managing Differences: How to Build Better Relationships at Work and Home*

All books are available at Amazon and other online booksellers.

Further details at Five Palms Press: dandana.us/fivepalms

I Got Off the Farm

in this life I've seen:
South Africa, Vietnam,
Japan, Honduras,

Peru, Uruguay,
Antarctica, Uganda,
Ukraine, Panama,

Israel, Qatar,
Lebanon, Ghana, Fiji,
Kenya, Korea,

Latvia, Hong Kong,
Australia, Brazil, Taiwan,
and most of Europe

why list these far lands*?
I simply want you to know
I got off the farm

* More than 85 total

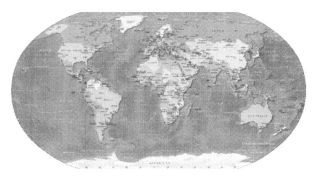

Image: Nations Online

"Travel is fatal to prejudice, bigotry, and narrow-mindedness."
　—Mark Twain

Antinatalism References

- Antinatalism International
  https://antinatalisminternational.com/what-is-antinatalism/
- Internet Encyclopedia of Philosophy
  https://iep.utm.edu/anti-natalism/
- Real Talk Philosophy
  https://www.realtalkphilosophy.org/antinatalism
- PhilArchive
  https://philarchive.org/archive/MORWIA-13
- The Ethics Centre
  https://ethics.org.au/anti-natalism-the-case-for-not-existing/
- American Ethical Union
  https://aeu.org/who-we-are/ethical-humanism/

Science References

Scientific assertions made in this book are generally noncontroversial findings in contemporary cosmology, biology, neurology, paleoanthrology, and other fields of research. Original sources may be found in corresponding topical pages in Wikipedia.

Acknowledgements

- Scribes, a Sarasota writers' group, particularly Aroon Chaddha, Martin Collins, Caitlyn Lincoln, Claire Matturro, Arvind Rajan, and Ann Trick.
- Humanists of Sarasota Bay, particularly Jim Bailey, Garrett Cantrell, Jack Davis, Holly Downing, Meigs Glidewell, Holly Gruenfeld, Michael Gruenfeld, David Helgager, Robert LaSalle, and Barry Zack
- Boffins: James Burns, MD and Darrel Ray, EdD
- Susan Dana, who frequently admonishes me to "not tell everything I know" yet somehow has supported me in this act of shameless self-disclosure
- Cover design by Chetan